D1616180

Written by
MELISSA
GARRICK
EDWARDS

CAN YOU SEE IF I'M A BEE?

Illustrated by
JONATHAN
WOODWARD

WITHDRAWN

DORRANCE
PUBLISHING CO
EST. 1920
PITTSBURGH, PENNSYLVANIA 15238

The contents of this work, including, but not limited to, the accuracy of events, people, and places depicted; opinions expressed; permission to use previously published materials included; and any advice given or actions advocated are solely the responsibility of the author, who assumes all liability for said work and indemnifies the publisher against any claims stemming from publication of the work.

All Rights Reserved
Copyright © 2021 by Melissa Garrick Edwards

No part of this book may be reproduced or transmitted, downloaded, distributed, reverse engineered, or stored in or introduced into any information storage and retrieval system, in any form or by any means, including photocopying and recording, whether electronic or mechanical, now known or hereinafter invented without permission in writing from the publisher.

Dorrance Publishing Co
585 Alpha Drive
Pittsburgh, PA 15238
Visit our website at www.dorrancebookstore.com

ISBN: 978-1-6480-4241-6
EISBN: 978-1-6480-4673-5

Can You See if I'm a Bee?

What is a bee? Let's find out why they are so important to you and me!

Bees

Bees are insects that are beneficial to plants.
They are close relatives of wasps and ants.

Because bees are insects, they have six legs,
Two eyes and two antennae on top of their heads.

A thorax and abdomen, which is like a belly,
But hard and stiff, not wiggly like jelly.

Bees have two pairs of wings; four wings in all
Strong enough to carry pollen that they need to haul.

Bees have a special place in their throats,
A crop to store pollen collected from places remote.

Bees undergo metamorphosis at different life stages.
This means that they change form at different ages.

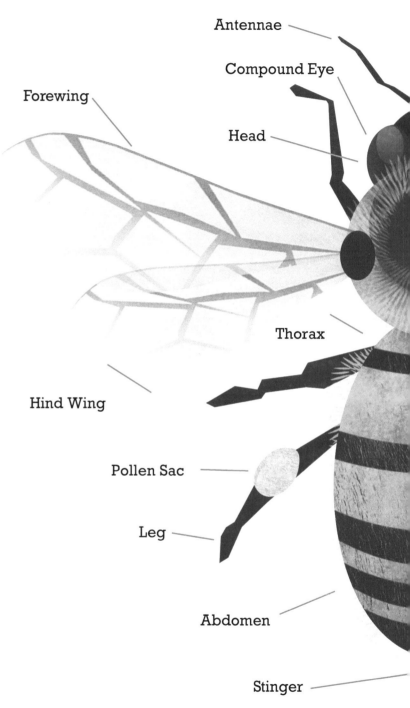

Antennae

Compound Eye

Forewing

Head

Thorax

Hind Wing

Pollen Sac

Leg

Abdomen

Stinger

A bee hatches from an egg as a larva,
A worm-like bug that changes into a pupa.

Pupae don't eat; they rest as they grow,
Then hatch as bees – who would have known?

Yes, bees are amazing insects, as you will discover —
They can fly forward, backward and sideways — even hover!

But the most incredible thing of all
Is how important they are, even though they are small.

Bees are the Best Pollinators

Some important information for everyone to know
Is that bees are the best pollinators of plants that grow.

Plants create new plants through pollination.
The following is a very important explanation!

From the biggest of trees to the smallest of weeds,
Plants create new plants by producing seeds.

Seeds are created when pollination occurs
When pollen moves from plant to plant, this is assured.

So how does pollen get from one plant to another?
By bees, one of nature's greatest wonders!

Bees drink sweet nectar from flowers for food,
Then collect pollen to bring to their brood.

Pollen sticks to their hairy legs
Or sometimes their bellies — and even their heads!

Then bees spread the pollen powder
When flying from flower to flower.

Bees help plants to reproduce
So they can grow fruit, vegetables and other produce.

Plants that make vegetables and fruits
Need bees to pollinate them – that is the scoop!

Bees are responsible for many things we need —
Medicines and beverages made from fruits and seeds.

Beeswax is used to make candles and crayons.
We wouldn't have clothes made out of cotton, but rayon.

They also make the honey that we eat,
Which is good for our health and makes a tasty treat.

There are native bees that have evolved over millions of years
In the countries where they first appeared.

This makes them very important for pollination
In the ecosystems of their nations.

Native bees and wildflowers are so closely linked
That without these bees, they would become extinct.

Because their bodies are specifically designed
To pollinate the plants that they find

They are also better in pollinating many crops
That the honeybee, which is from Europe, is not.

Now you know why bees are so important to us;
If they're gone we wouldn't have honey or enough fruit,
vegetables or nuts!

So now keep all of this in mind
And let's see how many bees you can find!

Am I a Bee?

Yes! I'm sure that you recognized me
Because I'm your typical honeybee.

Settlers brought my ancestors to North America over 400 years ago
To make honey and pollinate the crops they sowed.

I was also brought to many other nations
To help their farmers with crop pollination.

I am a very social bee who lives in a hive,
Where our queen and many other bees live and thrive.

The queen bee is the largest in our home,
Laying thousands of eggs fathered by drones.

Female worker bees like me
Are very busy; just look and see!

We build our honeycomb hives out of wax —
An amazing feat that no insect can match.

We make honey and gather nectar and pollen for food,
Tend the baby bees, the larvae and pupae, the "brood."

We protect the hive by stinging intruders,
Scaring away predators and other honey looters.

We can't talk, so we speak in a different way
By shaking our bodies to say what we want to say.

We dance to tell each other where the flowers are,
Whether they are near or very, very far.

7

Am I a Bee?

No, I'm a wasp and unlike a bumblebee I don't have much hair
So in that regard I'm really quite bare.

I also don't eat honey or pollen;
I like yummier foods, like things I find crawlin'!

By eating pesky insects, I help save food crops too;
However, this isn't all that I do!

I also like food that people eat —
So watch out! Your snack might make a tasty treat!

At summer picnics you will always find me munchin'.
I'm a nuisance, but I serve an important function.

By being a predator of many bad insects that eat crops for food,
So in that way, I do much good.

I really like nectar, fruit and most anything
But beware and watch out for my sting!

I am very aggressive and can be mean if crossed,
So stay away from me at any cost!

Am I a Bee?

Cuckoo Bee is my name and
The following is my claim to fame.

I'm a very sneaky bee;
I use other bees to raise my young for me.

I lay eggs in another bee's nest,
Sometimes eating her young before she can guess.

If I don't eat her eggs, mine will snatch
The other baby bees' food before they hatch.

Yes, they will eat the food that the mother bee has left
Without her realizing there has been a theft.

Or they might eat the baby bee eggs instead
Because they have big mandibles (jaws) attached to their heads.

So the poor mother bee will never know
That she and her brood helped my young ones grow!

Am I a Bee?

I might look like a bumblebee,
But I'm a robber fly who perches on plants and trees.

I look for flying insects of any kind —
Wasps, bees, dragonflies or whatever I can find.

I swoop out and grab my prey,
Holding on with strong legs to its dismay.

I bite and inject poison enzymes into its head;
Then I eat my meal after it is dead.

I'm a good killer of insect pests,
But I also eat bees along with the rest.

To a stinging insect prey's alarm,
I have a hairy face that protects me from harm.

Am I a Bee?

I'm a green sweat bee – what a strange name!
I'm smaller than a honeybee and I'm also quite tame.

I like to drink the salt in human sweat,
But don't worry, I'm not a threat.

I'm beautiful and shiny so I'm called the "flying jewel."
I fly from flower to flower, drinking nectar as fuel.

I collect pollen on my legs and take it to my nest
Where I usually live alone, but sometimes I have guests.

They are other female sweat bees of my kind
Where we share entrances of underground burrows that we find.

Am I a Bee?

I'm called a mason bee because I use mud to build a nest,
Creating partitions for my larvae to grow and rest.

Inside the hollow of a plant stem or an insect tunnel bored into wood,
I deposit pollen as food for my brood.

I am a solitary bee - I always live alone,
Not in hives that have many female bees and drones.

I hatch in early spring;
I'm very gentle and I don't like to sting.

I am a better pollinator than a honeybee —
That is why orchard farmers really like me.

I have a specialized way of pollinating certain plants
That native bees like me can do and honeybees can't.

I attach myself to a flower,
Then I use some of my mighty wings' muscle power.

I vibrate them and produce a peculiar sound
That causes the pollen grains to come loose and bounce up and down.

They gain so much energy because the sound is so loud;
The pollen bursts out of the anther tube as a pollen cloud.

When the pollen shoots out of the tube,
It coats my abdomen with wet clumps of pollen that I move

To another flowering plant close by
That I'll pollinate again using my specialized style.

This unique vibration of wing muscles and shaking
Is called "buzz pollination."

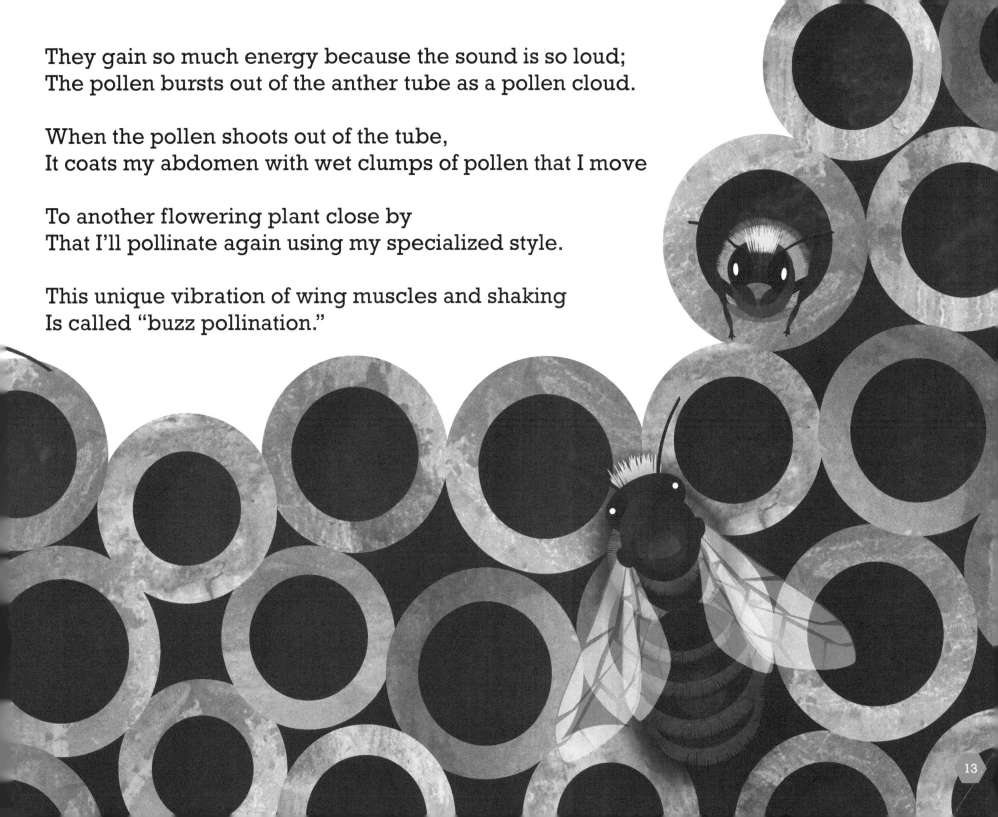

Am I a Bee?

I'm a female leafcutter bee
Who cuts shapes out of flowers or leaves from a tree.

Then I roll them into tubes to make a nest,
Where I lay my eggs to keep them safe from pests.

When my baby bees hatch in early spring,
They're full grown and will do the same thing.

Unlike most bees, my belly has hair
To carry pollen till I return to my lair.

This makes me easy to spot amongst other bees
Because most of them carry pollen on their legs and their knees.

Am I a Bee?

I'm not a bee, I'm a fly
It's the truth and not a lie.

I'm a fly that looks like a bee;
This is called "Batesian mimicry."

I'm harmless, but I copy a bee that can hurt
Keeping predators away and not becoming dessert!

You can tell I'm a fly because I have two wings,
My antennae are stubby and I also can't sting.

I am agile and like to fly quickly around;
I can land on the ceiling and walk upside down!

Yes, I have sticky feet and can walk anywhere
On slippery windows, mirrors or even a smooth chair.

Like bees, I'm a good pollinator too —
So did I fool most of you?

Am I a Bee?

Yes, I'm a bee. Can you guess what kind?
I will give you a hint — so keep this in mind!

I look very clumsy flying from flower to flower;
I just "bumble" along and "buzz" even louder.

I'm hairy with wide yellow and black stripes, you see —
Did you guess that I'm a bumblebee?

Sometimes we have orange or red stripes;
They're just part of my family of a different type.

I like to collect flower pollen for most of the day,
Even in low temperatures and light rain.

I collect a lot of pollen on my hind legs;
It looks like I am carrying yellow miniature eggs!

I don't live in a hive, I live underground;
Now how strange does that sound?

Our queen chooses an old rodent burrow or another sheltered place
So a small colony of bumblebees can live in a safe and secure space.

Am I a Bee?

I'm a male carder bee and I don't have a home,
But I try to claim a territory that I can call my own.

I have to protect it from other male bees
Who want to steal flower nectar from me.

They want to attract female bees too;
This is something that I don't want them to do.

So I try to chase them away.
This is what I do each and every day.

I'm not afraid of honey, bumbles or carpenter bees,
Even though they are much bigger than me.

If I can't make them leave, I hit them instead
With a hard "bonk" on the head.

That is why bee experts call me
The "head-bonker" bee!

Am I a Bee?

Surprise! I'm not a bee
But looking like one is important to me.

That way, birds and other insects won't think I'm a meal
So my camouflage gives me quite a good deal.

Something that you'll discover
Is that I really like to hover!

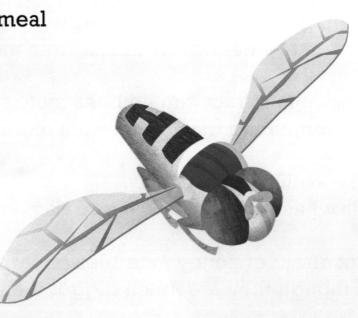

Just like a helicopter that can stay in one place,
I do the same while flying through space.

I also flit back and forth,
Moving quickly until I stop to hover of course!

So have you guessed my name?
I'm a hover fly and I'm very, very tame.

I'm not kidding you,
I pollinate plants just like bees do.

Female flies lay eggs on decaying waste;
When larvae hatch, they love its taste!

Before I grow up and turn into a fly
I'm a maggot on whom farmers can rely.

I eat bad insects such as aphids, thrips and grubs.
When I'm hungry, I try to catch each and every one.

Am I a Bee?

I'm one of the world's smallest bees.
In real life, you'd have a hard time seeing me.

I'm a dwarf honey bee, so small and thin
That I'm not much bigger than the head of a pin!

It is hard to believe that I'm usually found
By looking for my shadow as I pass along the ground.

Another amazing thing:
I'm a honeybee that doesn't sting.

My sisters and I protect our hive's honey
By coating intruders in sap till they shrivel into mummies.

I also protect our hive and fight
By giving any predators a nice big bite!

Am I a Bee?

I'm a mud dauber wasp,
Shiny and slender, black, brown, orange or yellow.

Sometimes I have black markings,
But I'm mostly a harmless fellow.

I look very mean and scary,
But I won't sting unless someone tries to hurt me or isn't being wary.

I love mud, which is how I got my name;
Females make nests out of it, which is our claim to fame.

They build nests in many places:
Under eaves, in attics, sheds and many other spaces.

Spiders and other bugs beware!
We hunt, paralyze and seal them in our lairs.

When dauber eggs hatch, the larvae have good food;
Spiders are always a welcome meal in our brood.

Am I a Bee?

I'm a carpenter bee and I dig a tunnel in wood
That becomes a nest for my brood.

I lay some eggs and bring them some food;
My larvae think plant pollen is very good.

I'm big, black and hairy;
I can also look and sound very scary.

Not only am I large and proud,
The hum of my wings is very loud.

Male bees of my kind
Protect our nests all of the time.

They fly towards intruders to scare them away
And they do it many times during the day.

But they are just pretending; they can't sting —
Because they don't have stingers, just very strong wings!

Am I a Bee?

Yes, I'm a male long-horned bee, and I look very strange.
My long antennae give me my name.

I am also hairy.
But I look cute, not scary!

Female bees are also covered in fuzz;
Around sunflowers and daisies, they are always a-buzz.

I can visit many flowers because I fly very fast;
So when it comes to quick pollination, the honeybee comes last!

Am I a Bee?

I'm a moth that looks like a bee
So that birds and other predators don't want to eat me.

My antennae are thick and look bent;
To mimic bees is my intent.

I'm just like bees that are black and yellow in color;
I'm also furry, as you will discover.

I have four wings like a bee —
Another way to fool predators, you see.

My wings are colored, not clear,
But when I fly these colors disappear!

So I look like a bee while in flight
Moving all four wings with all of my might.

I don't land on flowers like bees do;
I hover over them to collect my food.

I have a proboscis, a long slender tube
Which I use like straw to suck up nectar, my food.

My tongue is coiled under my head;
I roll it back up after I have fed.

Do All Bees Sting?

Most people think that all bees sting,
But not all of them do such a thing.

Sweat Bee

Did you know that male bees don't have stingers?
Many native bees won't sting unless you squeeze them between your fingers.

A queen honeybee can use her stinger again and again,
But will use it only if she has her life to defend.

Besides, she doesn't have to leave the nest.
The worker bees protect her and let her lay eggs and rest.

Bumblebee

Female honey and bumblebees don't like to sting 'cause they'll die.
So, unless they're protecting their hives, it's not worth a try.

But they will sting if threatened or attacked,
So if you see one, please stay back!

Just observe from a distance and you'll learn very much
And always remember not to touch.

It is very important to keep in mind
That you must be careful around stinging insects of all kinds.

What's The Bee Problem?

Bees are losing their environment —
To towns, cities, human homes and apartments.

They are dying from diseases and getting killed by parasites
Like the honeybees' enemy, the varroa mite.

Bees are accidentally exposed to poisonous pesticides
and other chemicals that were meant to kill pest insects.

We must help them in any way we can,
Even if we live in urban parts of the land.

Plant a garden at home in the ground or in a pot,
At school or an empty city lot.

Grow plants with various flowers which bloom at different times;
Then you will attract bees of many different kinds.

Don't use pesticides unless you really need to —
And if you must, choose products that don't kill bees too.

So let's be on Mother Nature's side
By helping bees and their ecosystems worldwide.

Now you can see that there are so many different kinds of bees!

Did you correctly guess which insects were bees?
Were you surprised that all don't live in hives or trees?

Now you know that bees come in many different shapes, sizes and colors
And that they behave quite differently from each other.

When honeybees come to mind,
You know that they are not all one of a kind.

Bumblebees aren't the only kinds of bees too;
And wasps look like bees, but now they won't fool you!

Native bees, like the mason or leafcutter bee,
Usually live alone, which means they are solitary.

Mason Bee

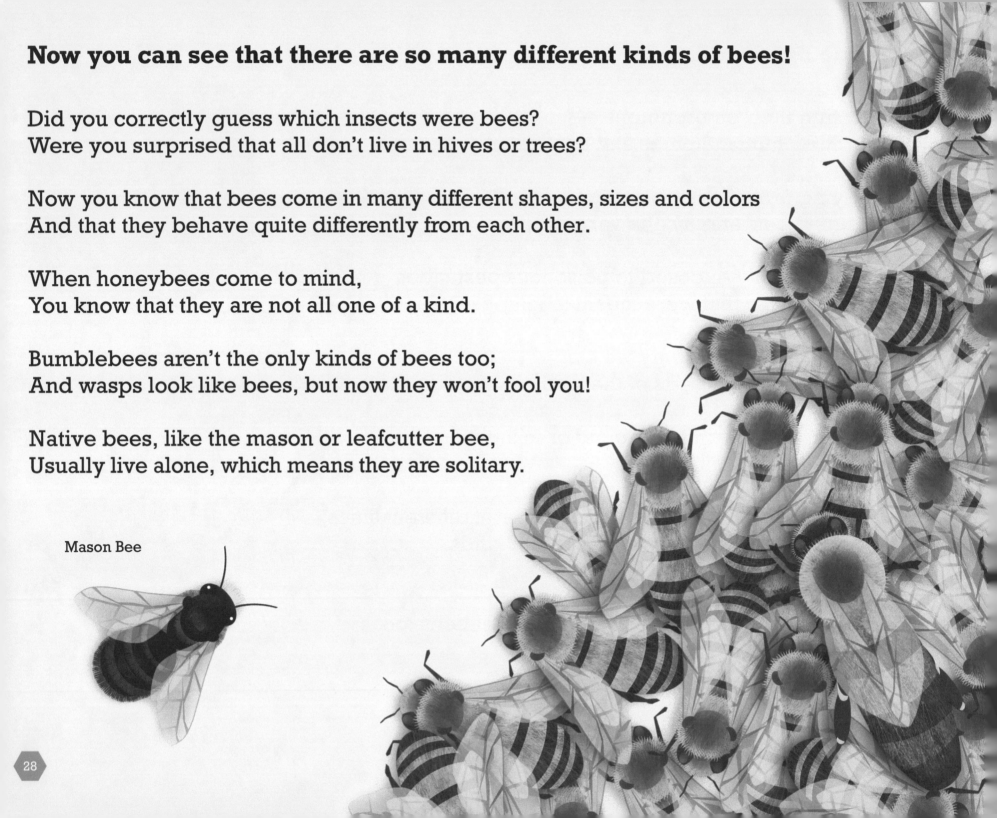

Some natives dig nests in the ground;
Others build theirs in existing holes in wood that they've found.

Honeybee and bumblebees live in hives;
Each bee has a job to do so that all of them thrive.

There are other bugs that look like them;
"Wanna" bees that can fool us every now and then.

Like the hover fly or the sphinx moth,
The yellow jacket or the mud-dauber wasp.

Yes, you've learned a lot —
Now there are many different types of bees that you can spot!

There are over 25,000 different kinds of bee species all over the world. This book has introduced you to some of them along with a few of their copycats.

Bees and Insects that Copy Them

EUROPEAN HONEYBEES make honey, which is how they got their name. Honeybees live together in nests called hives. There are thousands of bees per hive, sometimes up to 60,000 or more! Inside the hive is a wax honeycomb made of many hexagonally shaped spaces called cells. Some of these are used to store food (honey and pollen) and some are where the queen bee lays her eggs. There are other female bees in the hive, but they can't lay eggs. They are called "worker bees" because they build the honeycombs, gather food, make honey and take care of the baby bees or "brood" (eggs, larvae and pupae) before they hatch. They also protect the hive by stinging any predators that try to steal honey. The male bees of the hive are called drones. They are fed by the female worker bees. Also, they don't have stingers so they can't defend themselves or the hive; their only job is to father the baby bees.

BUMBLEBEES have a "bumbling" flight pattern, which is how they got their name. They are native bees, which means that they have always lived in their current environment and are therefore the best pollinators for their ecosystem because their bodies have specifically evolved to pollinate the plants that they visit. They are usually larger and rounder, with more hair than honeybees and are dark black with wide, yellow stripes. There are many different kinds of bumblebees with similar shapes, but different color patterns. Bumbles carry pollen on their hind legs, often in large yellow balls. They are one of the few kinds of native bees that are social, meaning they live together just like honeybees do. But they don't live in hives. Their nests are usually constructed in underground cavities, such as old mouse holes. The queen bumblebee has to start a nest on her own, unlike the queen honeybees which have help from large swarms of worker bees. Once a queen bumblebee's daughters are born, they help her finish the nest and take care of her and the rest of their family.

CARPENTER BEES look a lot like bumblebees except that they are usually much larger. There are also carpenter bees that are very small, smaller than some sweat bees. However, carpenter bees are usually all black or blue in color with a shiny metallic sheen; they also have little hair on their bodies. Carpenter bees construct nests in flower stalks or wood. Female carpenter bees construct long tunnels by chewing into solid wood where they lay their eggs and take care of them until they hatch. Carpenter bee eggs have the largest of all insect eggs. A female carpenter bee can lay an egg that is half her size! Large carpenter bees are very big and make a loud buzzing sound when they fly. Male bees hover around the tunnel entrances and frighten intruders away by zooming towards them. This is a good trick because male carpenter bees don't have stingers like the female bees do. Male bees try to chase people away from their territory, but they can't sting, so they never hurt anyone. Many people don't know this, so it scares them away anyway. Female bees hardly ever sting because if they do, they will die and won't be able to take care of their eggs.

LEAFCUTTER BEES got their name because females cut pieces off of leaves or flowers and use them to make their nests. They don't bother excavating their own nests, but find abandoned tunnels of wood-boring insects in dead limbs. They also use empty underground nests of rodents, hollow plant stems or almost any open hole they can find. They make nests inside these tunnels with the pieces of leaves or flowers that they have collected. Leafcutters are solitary bees, which means that they live alone and do not live in large groups or colonies like honeybees. Sometimes females will share a nest entrance even though they take care of their own nests. The largest bee in the world is the female leafcutter bee from Indonesia; she can grow to 39 millimeters or 1.5 inches in length.

MASON BEES are in the leafcutter bee family, but they do not build their nests with leaf pieces. These bees construct adobe-like nests out of mud in naturally occurring tubular cavities. Sometimes they make mud nests on top of rocks! Mason bees take care of their young by building nests and stockpiling them with food, which is a nutritious mixture of nectar, pollen and saliva. The female bee lays her egg in the nest and seals it in to keep it safe. Solitary bees do not feed and care for their growing young like honey and bumblebees do; they provide all of the food that their larvae will need to become adults. This is called "mass provisioning." Mason bees are shiny metallic blue-black in color and are smaller than honeybees. They are very good pollinators; just a few hundred mason bees can do the same work as tens of thousands of honeybees! They hatch in the early spring at the same time that many different kinds of fruit trees are flowering. That is why farmers use mason bees along with honeybees to pollinate their fruit tree orchards.

LONG-HORNED BEES get their name because the male bees have very long antennae. These bees are very robust with fuzzy yellow hairs. The female bee uses her hairy legs to carry pollen. Many of these bees like the flowers in the aster family, such as the daisy and sunflower. These flowers like these bees too, because many of them need these special bees to pollinate them. Most long-horned bees are solitary ground nesters. Some species nest communally, with several individuals using one burrow. They line their brood cells with a wax-like material they secrete. The wings often appear disproportionately short compared to other bees and their "buzz" is often a high-pitched whine as they hover and feed on flowers.

SWEAT BEES got their name because they like to lick salt off of sweaty skin and sometimes they will land on you. Fortunately, they are not aggressive, and they hardly ever sting. These native bees are small and easy to miss, but there are many around. There are many different kinds of sweat bees. Sweat bees are usually small, dark-colored bees with little hair. Most of them are brown or black, but the green or blue sweat bees are shiny and metallic in color. The green sweat bee has a bright, metallic green head and thorax with a striped abdomen. Some female bees are entirely bright green or blue. They build nests in the ground in deep abandoned rodent burrows, soil banks or rotting wood. They usually live alone, but sometimes they share nests even though each female bee still takes care of her own eggs and larvae. Because they are smaller than honeybees, they are hardly ever noticed and are often mistaken for small wasps or flies. Unlike honey and bumblebees, female sweat bees don't carry pollen neatly on their hind legs. They are "messy" pollen gatherers, not only carrying pollen on their front legs and back ones, but also on their sides and abdomen.

MALE CARDER BEES are very protective of their living spaces. Many male bees are territorial and patrol an area around the patch of flowers which is their food source. These flowers also attract the female carder bees, so the males try to chase each other away. The most aggressive male bee is the wool carder bee. He isn't afraid of anything. He'll attack honeybees, bumblebees and even large carpenter bees. Most of the time, the male wool carder bee will purposely fly into another male bee, knocking him off a flower. Ironically, during the night-time, after a hard day chasing each other away, male carder bees share the same flower for sleeping.

CUCKOO BEES are cleptoparasitic, which means they do not gather their own food or make nests themselves but use the nests and food of other types of bees to take care of their young. Cuckoo bees sneak into the nests of other bees and lay their eggs. When the young cuckoo bees hatch, they eat the food that was meant for the host bee's larvae. Sometimes they even eat the eggs or the larvae of the host female bee. Cuckoo bees will also kill a queen bee in her nest and then lay their own eggs where the queen bee's eggs were supposed to go. This forces the dead queen bee's workers to raise young parasitic bees without even knowing that they are doing so. The cuckoo bee doesn't have a lot of hair, so many people confuse it with wasps like the yellow jacket. They don't need any pollen-collecting hairs on their bodies because they don't have to collect pollen and nectar for their young.

DWARF OR STINGLESS HONEYBEES are from tropical or warmer parts of the world. Africa, Australia, Mexico, Central and South America are some of the places where they live. Dwarf honeybees are similar to European honeybees in many ways. They live inside hives with a queen, drones and many female worker bees. They are different from honeybees in that they do not sting or make very much honey. Because predators like ants, flies and beetles try to eat their honey, dwarf honeybees have to defend their nests in creative ways. They close all openings to their hive except for a small entrance hole. If a predator enters the hive, dwarf bees bite or secrete acid that can dissolve the hard shells of insects. Sometimes they cover intruders with a sticky mix of tree sap, mud and wax that can turn them into miniature mummies!

Bee Mimics

Here are some of the insects that might have fooled you and made you think that they are bees. This is called "Batesian mimicry," which is nature's way of protecting harmless insects to keep them safe from predators that would otherwise eat them.

YELLOW JACKETS are wasps, not bees. They are relatives of bees, so they are very similar in appearance and behavior. Like honeybees, they live in big colonies that has one queen and many worker wasps. They make nests out of wood or plant fiber that they collect and chew up. Some kinds of yellow jackets build football-shaped nests and hang them from trees or other overhead structures like the eaves on buildings. Other types of yellow jackets build their nests in underground tunnels made by other creatures such as rodents or snakes or they make their nests inside of hollow trees. Yellow jackets are very aggressive, which means that they get upset very easily and will chase and sting over and over again because they don't lose their stingers and die like honeybees do. So stay away from yellow jackets or you are likely to get some very painful stings!

MUD DAUBER WASPS are in a different family than yellow jackets and other wasps; unlike their relatives, they don't live together in a large colony. Instead, they build individual nests near other mud dauber wasps. They make their nests out of mud, making long clay tubes or lumps that they put in protected places like sheds, attics, house siding or under porch ceilings. Mud daubers prey on other insects, paralyzing them with their stings. They provide food for their larvae by putting their insect prey inside of the mud nests that they build. Even though mud dauber wasps can deliver a nasty sting, they are not aggressive and will leave people alone unless someone tries to hold or hurt them.

HOVER OR DRONE FLIES got their name because they stay very still while flying, hovering in one place for several seconds or more. Even though they look and sound similar to bees when they are flying, their behavior is very different. Not only do they hover in one place for a long time, they'll suddenly fly away, moving very quickly, darting here and there and then suddenly stopping to hover in one place again. Like bees, hover flies drink nectar and eat pollen as well as pollinate plants (although not as well as bees do). Hoverfly larvae (which are called maggots) eat dead plant or decaying animal matter in the soil or in ponds and streams. Sometimes larvae eat aphids, thrips and other plant-sucking insects that kill plants, making them vital in getting rid of pests that can harm or kill many food crops.

BEE FLIES are also commonly mistaken for bees. They are stout-bodied, yellow-haired flies that can be seen hovering or even resting on flowers on sunny days. While resting, they hold their wings outstretched like those on an airplane, whereas bees tuck theirs together above their abdomens. Bee fly legs are thin and don't have any hairs on them to carry pollen. They drink nectar from flowers. They are able to enter the brooding chambers of the ground nesting bees that they mimic and lay their eggs there. When they hatch, the larvae feed on the bee eggs and the food that was provisioned for them. Fortunately, there are other species of bee fly that do this to insects which are destructive to plants.

ROBBER FLIES are another of nature's Batesian "mimics" which are also mistaken for bees. The best way to tell the difference between a robber fly and a bee is to look at the wings: flies have only two wings, whereas bees have four. Considered beneficial insects, robber flies eat many bugs that destroy plants. Unfortunately, some robber fly species eat bees and other good insects too. As sad as this may seem, it is all a part of Mother Nature's plan to keep everything in the natural world in balance.

HUMMINGBIRD OR SPHINX MOTHS hover over flowers just like hummingbirds do, which is how they got their name. They are naturally camouflaged to look like bees so that insect predators which hunt them for food won't touch them. This allows these moths to fly during the day to collect their food instead of at night like most moths do. They hover over their favorite flowers and feed by drinking nectar with their very long tongues (proboscises), which is similar to humans drinking out of a straw. Hummingbird moths only look like bees while in flight; when they land, their large wings stay spread out. Decorated with different patterns that help them blend into their environment, the wings of a hummingbird moth make it difficult for them to be seen by predators.

With Special
thanks to

**Dr. Vicki
Wojcik**

POLLINATOR
PARTNERSHIP

Protect their lives. Preserve ours.

www.pollinator.org

CPSIA information can be obtained
at www.ICGtesting.com
Printed in the USA
BVHW090623230322
631699BV00001B/6

CONTRA COSTA COUNTY LIBRARY

31901068003849